P9-ANY-686

Publisher's note:

Tintin, the intrepid reporter, first made his appearance January 10, 1929, in a serial newspaper strip with an adventure in the Soviet Union. From there, it was on to the Belgian Congo and then to America. Together with his dog, Snowy; an old seaman, Captain Haddock; an eccentric professor, Cuthbert Calculus; look-alike detectives, Thomson and Thompson; and others, Tintin roamed the world from one adventure to the next.

Tintin's dog, Snowy, a small white fox terrier, converses with Tintin, saves his life many times, and acts as his confidant, despite his weakness for whiskey and a tendency toward greediness. Captain Haddock, in some ways Snowy's counterpart, is a reformed lover of whiskey, with a tendency toward colorful language and a desire to be a gentleman-farmer. Cuthbert Calculus, a hard-of-hearing, sentimental, absent-minded professor, goes from small-time inventor to nuclear physicist. The detectives, Thomson and Thompson, stereotyped characters down to their old-fashioned bowler hats and outdated expressions, are always chasing Tintin. Their attempts at dressing in the costume of the place they are in make them stand out all the more.

The Adventures of Tintin appeared in newspapers and books all over the world. Georges Remi (1907–1983), better known as Hergé, based Tintin's adventures on his own interest in and knowledge of places around the world. The stories were often irreverent, frequently political and satirical, and always exciting and humorous.

Tintin's Travel Diaries is a new series, inspired by Hergé's characters and based on notebooks Tintin may have kept as he traveled. Each book in this series takes the reader to a different country, exploring its geography, and the customs, the culture, and the heritage of the people living there. Hergé's original cartooning is used, juxtaposed with photographs showing the country as it is today, to give a feeling of fun as well as education.

If Hergé's cartoons seem somewhat out of place in today's society, think of the time in which they were drawn. The cartoons reflect the thinking of the day, and set next to modern photographs, we learn something about ourselves and society, as well as about the countries Tintin explores. We can see how attitudes have changed over the course of half a century.

Hergé, himself, would change his stories and drawings periodically to reflect the changes in society and the comments his work would receive. For example, when it was originally written in 1930, *Tintin in the Congo*, on which *Tintin's Travel Diaries: Africa* is based, was slanted toward Belgium as the fatherland. When Hergé prepared a color version in 1946, he did away with this slant. Were Hergé alive today, he would probably change many other stereotypes that appear in his work.

From the Congo, Tintin went on to America. This was in 1931. Al Capone was notorious, and the idea of cowboys and Indians, prohibition, the wild west, as well as factories, all held a place of fascination. *Cigars of the Pharaoh* (1934) introduced Hergé's fans to the mysteries of Egypt and India. A trip to China came with *The Blue Lotus* in 1936, the first story Hergé thoroughly researched. After that, everything was researched, including revisions of previous stories. *The Land of Black Gold*, for example, an adventure in the Middle East, was written in 1939, and revised in 1949 and again in 1969. *The Black Island*, Tintin's adventure in Scotland, was published in black and white in 1938, in color in 1943, and updated in 1965. *Tintin in Tibet* began later. It came out in book form in 1960, thoroughly researched, down to the Yeti!

Although *The Broken Ear* introduced readers to the Amazon region in 1935, the story was pure fantasy, complete with imaginary countries. In 1974 the adventure continued with *Tintin and the Picaros*, Hergé's last story. When *The Seven Crystal Balls*, which was serialized from 1943 to 1944, was continued in 1946, Hergé began to give the reader factual information about pre-Columbian civilization with marginal notes titled "Who were the Incas?" *Tintin in the Land of the Soviets* was Tintin's first adventure, in 1929, and the only one not to be redone in color.

Tintin's Travel Diaries are fun to read, fun to look at, and provide educational, enjoyable trips around the world. Perhaps, like Tintin, you, too, will be inspired to seek out new adventures!

The publisher particularly wishes to thank Mrs. Christine Ockrent and television channel Antenne 2 for their kind permission to use the title *Travel Diaries*.

SCOTLAND

TINTIN'S TRAVEL DIARIES

A collection conceived and produced by Martine Noblet.

CD BR
J
DA762
.B713
1995

GOODMAN SQUARE

MAR   1996

Les films du sable thank the following **Connaissance du monde** photographers for their participation in this work:

Jean-Louis Mathon, Luc Giard, Maximilien Dauber

The authors thank Christiane Erard and Chantal Deltenre for their collaboration.

First edition for the United States and Canada published
by Barron's Educational Series, Inc., 1995.

© Copyright 1995 by Barron's Educational Series, Inc.,
with respect to the English language translation.
© Copyright 1992 by Hergé-Moulinsart
© Copyright 1992 by Casterman, Tournai, for the original edition.

All rights reserved.
No part of this book may be reproduced in any form,
by photostat, microfilm, xerography, or any other means,
or incorporated into any information retrieval system,
electronic or mechanical, without the written permission
of the copyright owner.

All inquiries should be addressed to:
Barron's Educational Series, Inc.
250 Wireless Boulevard
Hauppauge, New York 11788

Library of Congress Catalog Card No. 95-12370

International Standard Book No. 0-8120-6503-4 (hardcover)
International Standard Book No. 0-8120-9238-4 (paperback)

Library of Congress Cataloging-in-Publication Data

Bruycker, Daniel de.
    [Ecosse. English]
    Scotland / text by Daniel de Bruycker and Maximilien Dauber ; translation by Maureen
Walker. — 1st ed.
      p.   cm. — (Tintin's travel diaries)
    Includes bibliographical references and index.
    ISBN 0-8120-6503-4 (hardcover). — ISBN 0-8120-9238-4 (pbk.)
    1. Scotland—Juvenile literature.   [1. Scotland.]   I. Hergé, 1907–   II. Dauber,
Maximilien.   III. Walker, Maureen.   IV. Title.   V. Series.
DA762.B713 1995
941.1—dc20
                                                                                    95-12370
                                                                                    CIP
                                                                                    AC

Printed in Hong Kong
5678   9927   987654321

SCOTLAND

Text by Daniel De Bruycker and Maximilien Dauber

Translation by Maureen Walker

BARRON'S

It happened one morning. Oh, not an ordinary morning—no, indeed!—but a June morning in 1962. I was about to get on the train to go to my grandparents' house, where I was to spend my vacation. I remember everything about it—my mother fussing around me checking for the hundredth time that all was in order, my beret clamped firmly on my head, my short pants perfect, and my cologne-soaked handkerchief folded in my right pocket. Under the vast, glass-paned roof of the Lyon train station, the acrid smell of coal was everywhere. I liked disappearing in the clouds of steam escaping from the huge locomotives waiting on the tracks. These special moments made me happy, because going away always meant there'd be a stop at the newspaper stand.

That particular morning, I remember, was when I met one who would become my hero—Tintin, with his companion Snowy, in *The Unicorn's Secret*. He embodied not only imagination, humor, and adventure but kindness, friendship, and humanity as well. These diffuse feelings clashed in my childish heart; reality was easier to deal with. To the eternal question, "What are you going to do, when you grow up?" I used to answer, "I'll be a traveler, like Tintin." Little by little, the years go by, but he's always there, beside me—they're all there, Tintin and his buddies. Even better, today I'm fulfilling the best of my childhood dreams—meeting Tintin again on my latest trip to Scotland.

JEAN-LOUIS MATHON

Hi there, big brother!

Tintin the ingenious, the death-defying, forever ready to serve a noble cause—who hasn't dreamed of taking part in your adventures someday? You proved to me that anything is possible; so, without even wondering about it, I followed you, with my camera at the ready, to capture in my turn the world's treasures.

The fleeting richness of experience, encounters with other human beings, other customs, other landscapes, were feasts shared with friends on returning or kept in mind to improve my life.

I've been around the world twenty times and never once met you. But you pointed out the way so well that everything has turned out perfectly. And it's not over yet . . .

LUC GIARD

CONTENTS

The words in **boldface** refer to the glossary, beginning on page 70.

WHERE IS SCOTLAND?

1

Scotland is part of Europe and, together with England, Wales, and Northern Ireland, makes up one country, called the United Kingdom of Great Britain and Northern Ireland. But it was not always so.

For centuries, Scotland was perceived as a "land of the Far North," distant, wild, and little known—a country of legend. In ancient times, Greek and Phoenician sailors, who went as far away as **Cornwall** to look for zinc ore, knew Scotland only from the tales of the natives—stories about wild, barren lands where the sun scarcely rose in winter. Legends evoked ferocious warriors—**Druids**, possessed of vast powers—and all sorts of creatures, such as fairies and **elves**, who, so it was said, haunted these misty, wind-buffeted coasts.

At that time, many people were unaware that lands existed even farther north, and fantastic Scotland was known as "ultima Thule"—the last land before the icy solitude of the polar seas.

That was not entirely false: Indeed, nearly 12,000 years ago, Scotland lay beneath a thick ice cap, as Greenland does today. Scottish landscapes still bear traces of it: The marks of the glaciers of long ago can be found even today. Glaciers planed down the mountains, exposing large areas of rock, and cut into the coastline, hollowing out deep fjords, long arms of the sea that the Scots call firths. And the glaciers formed steeply banked lakes, known as lochs, in the bottoms of the valleys.

Top: Brander Pass
Bottom: Plockton, north of Kyle of Lochalsh

HOW DID SCOTLAND GET ITS NAME?

Scotland means "land of the Scots." The Scots were a Celtic, or Gaelic-speaking, people, of the same family as the Gauls who populated France. Arriving from Ireland, they settled in Scotland in the sixth century after the birth of Christ.

The Scots were not the first inhabitants of the country that bears their name today. On landing, they had to drive back toward the north another people, the **Picts**, who had themselves succeeded other populations, even more ancient. Almost nothing is known of the very first inhabitants of Scotland, except that they erected megalithic monuments, called **cairns**, and set up the lines of upright stones that can still be seen along the coasts.

Scotland was also called Caledonia, a name given it by the Romans. The Picts, a powerful, organized people, had their kings, their gods, and their priests (the Druids). They raised cattle and knew how to forge iron and gold. But divided into nations, then into tribes, and then into families (the clans), they were unable to stand up to the powerful military machine of the Roman legions. Little by little, they were forced back toward the north and into the islands, making way for the settlement of the Scots.

While the inhabitants of southern Britain took up the Christian faith very early, the Scots in the north remained steeped in their own traditions. Gaelic, the language of **bards**, who chanted wondrous tales of gods and heroes to the accompaniment of harp and bagpipes, is still spoken in some areas.

Top: Standing Stones of Callanish in the Hebrides
Bottom: Cemetery with Gaelic crosses
Bottom right: Kidalton Cross, Islay

WHO BUILT THE LONGEST WALL IN EUROPE?

Although the Romans conquered the British Isles, they never succeeded in subduing the Scots. To protect himself from their incursions, the emperor Hadrian built a wall that was 73 miles (117 km) long!

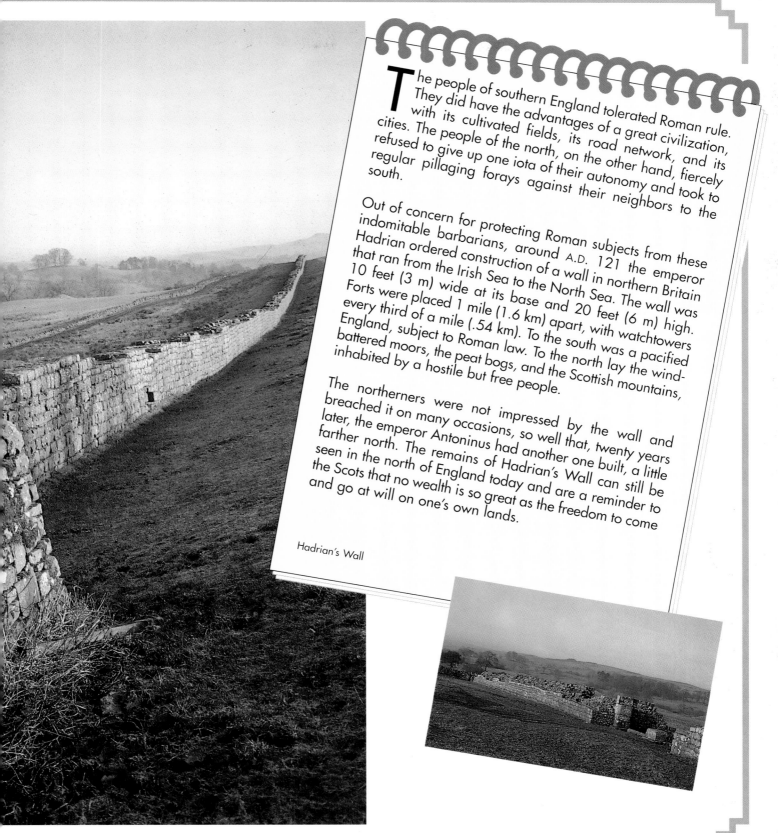

The people of southern England tolerated Roman rule. They did have the advantages of a great civilization, with its cultivated fields, its road network, and its cities. The people of the north, on the other hand, fiercely refused to give up one iota of their autonomy and took to regular pillaging forays against their neighbors to the south.

Out of concern for protecting Roman subjects from these indomitable barbarians, around A.D. 121 the emperor Hadrian ordered construction of a wall in northern Britain that ran from the Irish Sea to the North Sea. The wall was 10 feet (3 m) wide at its base and 20 feet (6 m) high. Forts were placed 1 mile (1.6 km) apart, with watchtowers every third of a mile (.54 km). To the south was a pacified England, subject to Roman law. To the north lay the wind-battered moors, the peat bogs, and the Scottish mountains, inhabited by a hostile but free people.

The northerners were not impressed by the wall and breached it on many occasions, so well that, twenty years later, the emperor Antoninus had another one built, a little farther north. The remains of Hadrian's Wall can still be seen in the north of England today and are a reminder to the Scots that no wealth is so great as the freedom to come and go at will on one's own lands.

Hadrian's Wall

ARE THE SCOTS ENGLISH?

4

Whatever you do, never call a Scot English! Even though Scotland has been part of the United Kingdom since 1707, the Scots draw pride and identity from their long history as an independent nation and keep alive the memory of harsh conflicts with their English opponents.

North of Hadrian's Wall, the Scots and the Picts lived for a long time in their own way, divided into clans led by chiefs. Around the eighth century, Vikings from Scandinavia came ashore from their **drakkars** and began to get a foothold on the islands north and west of Scotland. The inhabitants realized they would have to unite, and in 843 (in the time of the early Middle Ages), Kenneth McAlpin founded the first Scottish kingdom. But the danger was not only in the north and the west but also in the south, from England. On the battle-fields, the Scots were a good match for the English, but the more refined ways of the southerners gradually won over first the court of the king of Scotland and then the nobles and the priests.

In 1286, Alexander III, king of Scotland, died without an heir. Edward I, king of England, then seized Scotland and crushed a first rebellion led by **Sir William Wallace**. The Scots regained their independence in 1328, with **Robert Bruce** being recognized as King Robert I. Then began a period in which the Scottish monarchy formed alliances with France (this was during the Hundred Years' War, which brought France into conflict with England). The famous *Auld Alliance*, or "Old Alliance," thus enabled Scottish soldiers to fight alongside Joan of Arc.

Scottish people

WHAT ARE THE "HIGHLANDS" AND THE "LOWLANDS"?

Scotland has three main geographic regions: the Highlands in the north, with its rugged terrain; the Central Lowlands, with its fertile valleys; and the Southern Uplands, with its rolling moors.

Through much of the Middle Ages, visitors to Scotland noticed few differences between the Highlands and the Lowlands. Scotland seemed an exotic, primitive land, where people spoke a foreign language, Gaelic; lived in clans; and wore an exotic clothing, the plaid. Only in the late Middle Ages did that begin to change, as Scottish Lowlanders in the vicinity of the court began to speak a new language, Scots, a close relative of the English language spoken south of the border. Gradually, Lowlanders began to separate themselves from the Highlanders in religion, manners, and dress. They would eventually establish separate loyalties as well.

During the sixteenth century, Scotland and England began to draw closer together. The death of England's Queen Elizabeth I without children in 1603 left James VI of Scotland as heir to the English throne. Neither he nor his descendants were successful at ruling the two kingdoms together, and they suffered rebellions during the 1640s and again in the 1680s, when the **Stuarts** were finally driven from the throne. That was followed in 1707 with the Act of Union, uniting England and Scotland by treaty.

Many Highlanders remained loyal to the Stuarts, and they rose in rebellion in 1688, 1715, and 1745. The last of those rebellions was followed by the devastation of the Highlands by government troops led by the **Duke of Cumberland**. That was followed by one of the first emigrations of Highlanders from Scotland, repeated many times since. Today, the descendants of those emigrants can be found as far away as the United States, Canada, Australia, and New Zealand.

Top: Dunnottar Castle
Bottom: Rugged beauty of the Highlands

WHAT IS THE RELIGION OF SCOTLAND?

Christianity originally united the Scots. But it later became a source of discord, when the inhabitants of the Lowlands became Protestant, whereas most Highlanders remained Catholic.

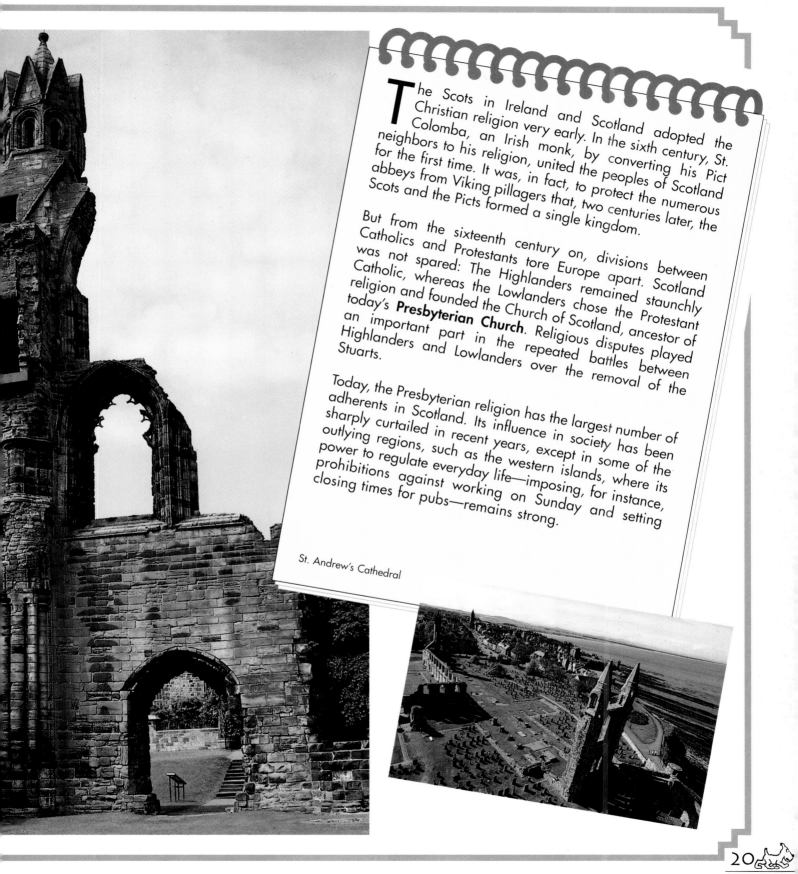

The Scots in Ireland and Scotland adopted the Christian religion very early. In the sixth century, St. Colomba, an Irish monk, by converting his Pict neighbors to his religion, united the peoples of Scotland for the first time. It was, in fact, to protect the numerous abbeys from Viking pillagers that, two centuries later, the Scots and the Picts formed a single kingdom.

But from the sixteenth century on, divisions between Catholics and Protestants tore Europe apart. Scotland was not spared: The Highlanders remained staunchly Catholic, whereas the Lowlanders chose the Protestant religion and founded the Church of Scotland, ancestor of today's **Presbyterian Church**. Religious disputes played an important part in the repeated battles between Highlanders and Lowlanders over the removal of the Stuarts.

Today, the Presbyterian religion has the largest number of adherents in Scotland. Its influence in society has been sharply curtailed in recent years, except in some of the outlying regions, such as the western islands, where its power to regulate everyday life—imposing, for instance, prohibitions against working on Sunday and setting closing times for pubs—remains strong.

St. Andrew's Cathedral

WAS SCOTLAND EVER RULED BY CHILDREN?

The history of the kings of Scotland is a succession of dramatic events. Many of these sovereigns died young, abandoning the throne to children incapable of defending it!

In the Stuart family, most of the kings who came to the throne were under ten years old. **Mary Stuart**, for instance, became queen when she was just six days old! Few of them survived beyond age forty.

But the Scots still cling to the turbulent past of their monarchy, despite some very bad memories—Mary Stuart, imprisoned because of her religious scheming, or Charles Edward Stuart ("Bonnie Prince Charlie"), whom the Highlanders tried unsuccessfully to restore to the throne in 1745 and who had to flee disguised as a maid, abandoning his country to the wrath of the Duke of Cumberland's soldiers.

With the great barons who headed the struggle against the English—such as Robert Bruce or Sir William Wallace—the child-kings of Scotland remained heroes of national legend, facing the "tyrants and oppressors" who wanted to punish the country for its desire for independence. And today, as many Scots seek greater control of their own affairs within the United Kingdom, nobody forgets the great figures of the past.

Left: Mary Stuart
Right: Queen Elizabeth

WHAT IS THE CAPITAL OF SCOTLAND?

Dominated by its impressive castle, Edinburgh, with its palace, its abbeys, and its university, has not forgotten that it was long the capital of an independent kingdom.

In Scottish, Edinburgh means "Edwin's castle," from the name of the king who, more than 1,000 years ago, had his fortress built on the rocky spur overlooking the site. As capital of the kings of Scotland, the city includes a fine palace (Holyrood), two ancient abbeys, and one of the foremost universities in Great Britain. Even though Edinburgh has not been home to a sovereign for nearly four centuries, the city still has the appearance of a capital city, with its museums, fine residential areas, and important economic and banking activity. Spared the ravages of industry, it is still an elegant city of romantic charm; it is also Scotland's second largest city, after Glasgow.

Many famous people have been born there, such as Alexander Graham Bell, inventor of the telephone, and Robert Louis Stevenson, author of the classic novel Treasure Island.

There are two ways to find out about Edinburgh. One is to stroll through the old city, where remarkable monuments and ancient houses are reminders of a prestigious past. The other is to visit the lively modern city at the end of August, when the Edinburgh Festival is held. This event attracts musical shows from all over the world, as well as concerts, drama, dance, poetry, jazz, and film. One evening in August should be set aside to attend the Tattoo, the great military parade that takes place to the sound of the bagpipes on the grounds of the castle.

Edinburgh

WHERE IS THE BLACK ISLE?

Most of the islands off the coast of Scotland are located to the west, such as the Hebrides, or to the north, such as the Orkneys and the Shetlands. But on the east coast of Scotland, north of Inverness, is a peninsula known as Black Isle.

The Hebrides, sanctuary of **Celtic** tradition, are large, rocky islands where the soil is as poor as it is in the Highlands. Today, a fleet of vessels shuttles between this archipelago and the mainland, but for a long time, the inhabitants lived isolated from the world, cultivating the ancient customs of Gaelic Scotland. Fishers still take to sea in tiny cockleshells of boats, defying the currents and dangerous whirlpools. The host of lighthouses dotted along these coasts have not averted numerous shipwrecks off the ragged coasts of Scotland and Ireland.

The Orkneys and the Shetlands, long dominated by the Vikings from Denmark and Norway, almost seem like part of Scandinavia. Harsh and nearly untillable, they are heavily populated by myriad seabirds and several species of seal. Although operating the North Sea oil fields has brought in a few visiting technicians, the islands' main resources are still fishing and, in particular, sheep farming. Along with wool from the island of Harris (in the Hebrides), wool from the Shetlands is the most appreciated; today, it is world-famous.

Top: Eoligarry, Barra Island, Hebrides
Bottom: Shipwreck run aground
Right: Seal in the Shetland Islands

WHO HAS SEEN THE LOCH NESS MONSTER?

Does a mysterious monster really haunt the dark waters of Loch Ness? Reporters and scientists from all over the world have followed in each other's footsteps on the shores of the lake, but none has ever been able to prove—or disprove—the existence of "Nessie."

It's as hard not to believe in the Loch Ness monster as it is to truly believe in it! It was already being talked about 1,400 years ago, when St. Colomba was preaching in Scotland. It's a fact that there has been much more talk about it since the opening of a highway in 1933. As if by coincidence, the "sightings" have become more numerous, attracting ever increasing numbers of sightseers and tourists to the shores of the loch. "Lots of people have seen it!" asserts one group. "Stuff and nonsense!" retorts another. "And then, what with the whisky, you know . . ." "Some people have managed to get photos!" claim the most tenacious ones. "But the pictures are so fuzzy," the skeptics reply, "and of such poor quality that they could be of anything!" And so the discussion goes on, to the great joy of seekers of curiosity, lovers of the fantastic, and, of course, sellers of souvenirs.

At least one of the photographs of Nessie has been exposed as a hoax. The famous photograph shown here was made from a child's windup submarine fitted with a foot-long (30.48 cm) plastic neck.

Still, Loch Ness is worth a side trip. There are the deep gray, peaty waters to be seen, tucked in between wooded slopes from which mysterious castles suddenly emerge. And then you realize that if there is a monster, it chose a good lair.

Above: Castle Stalker, Appin, Argyllshire   Inset: "Nessie." This photo was revealed in 1944 to have been a hoax by the man who set it up.

WHAT IS A "SCOTTISH SHOWER"?

"In Scotland, it rains every day," some people say. "Not at all!" reply others. "It's always fine!" There's no way to decide between them, because Scotland has the most unstable weather patterns imaginable. Now rain, now sun—that's a "Scottish shower."

Scotland is subject to two climates. From the west, from the Atlantic Ocean crossed by the **Gulf Stream**, come mild, humid winds that allow even warm-climate plants to grow. In the east, however, cold, dry winds from Norway move across the coast.

Scotland is located at the meeting place of these two climates, hence the proverbially unstable weather. At the slightest puff of wind, moist air meets cold, and just when the sky seemed blue, it suddenly starts to rain. Another puff of wind and the clouds part again, as if by magic, until the next whim of the weather. It's hardly surprising, then, that the raincoat was invented by a man named Macintosh.

The Scots have a philosophical outlook and have learned to make light of the capricious climate. They'll tell you, "When you can see **Ben Nevis** on the horizon, it's going to rain; when you can't see it, it's raining already!" And some will add, "How could we distill such good whisky if we didn't have all this fresh water?"

Left: Fishing near the Isle of Skye
Right: Sheep in the Highlands

HOW IS WHISKY MADE?

Stream water, barley, peat fires—and Scottish magic—give this country and the world at large a truly famous drink. It is to be consumed, preferably, in moderation!

In the beginning, it was not the Scots but the Irish who invented whiskey (the word is actually of Gaelic origin and means *aqua vitae*, or water of life). Probably St. Colomba's monks, arriving long ago to evangelize Scotland, brought it with them. But nobody today denies that some of the world's best whisky* is distilled in Scotland's whisky regions, such as the Spey Valley, in the heart of the Highlands.

The recipe? Leave barleycorns to soak for several days in pure Scottish river water. Stop germination when it starts by heating the grain over a peat fire, this process giving the future drink its smoky flavor. Crush the grain and brew it in water to obtain a "wort" to which yeast is added. Fermentation then produces a liquid, which, after two or three distillations in huge copper stills, makes whisky. Then the aging period begins: The alcohol, generally stored in oaken barrels impregnated with Portuguese wine, will slowly acquire its famous amber color from contact with the wood. After about eight to fifteen years of waiting, it is bottled.

Whisky is a strong alcohol, one best not abused. But drinking it at the end of a long walk in the rain, in the cozy atmosphere of a Scottish pub, is comforting.

*Whiskey or whisky? In Scotland, it's always *whisky*!

Distillation room of Glenfiddich in Dufftown

WHAT IS THE EMBLEM OF SCOTLAND?

The Scots could have chosen a sheep as their emblem. But that peaceful animal has nothing in common with the somewhat rough character of the Scots, so they selected the thistle instead: Anyone who bumps into it gets pricked!

Thistle can be found along the purple moors of the Highlands, but it is not indigenous to Scotland. Legend has it that invading Danes stepped on a bed of thistles and cried out in pain, thus warning the Gaels, who then put them to flight. The spiny plant thrives amid the rhododendrons, whose blossoms mark the return of spring, and the spiny shrubs known as broom and gorse. It towers above the heather that carpets the landscape with a mantle of mauve and pink in summer and autumn.

Though the Lowlands are covered with great dark forests, trees are sparse in the Highlands and islands. The wind blows too strongly there, and the arable land is often merely a thin layer covering rock, which surfaces in places. Extensive outcropping of granite and pink sandstone still bears scars left from the scraping of the great glaciers that covered Scotland 12,000 years ago.

Thistles and heather, a few black-faced sheep grazing in semifreedom, and the clouds heralding the next downpour bring to mind the wild landscape so dear to the Scottish soul. Such romantic scenery has always attracted travelers capable of enjoying it on their long, solitary rambles.

Thistles in the Highlands

WHAT STRANGE FOODS ARE EATEN IN SCOTLAND?

In an austere country often harsh to live in, the Scots have managed to make the best use of its meager resources. So they prepare a few typical dishes that are, to say the least, unusual.

The Scots are very proud of their haggis and gently make fun of the worried looks of their guests while they are explaining how the dish is prepared. You take a sheep's maw and stuff it with the sheep's intestines, kidneys, heart, and lungs, combined with a few onions that have been mixed with some oatmeal to bind them, and then you cook it. Of course its look and aroma are not much more encouraging than the explanation of the recipe—but the result is a delicious, flavorful dish that is always served with turnips (neeps)!

Another way of using up leftovers gave us orange marmalade. Nowadays, it is found on every British breakfast table and indeed around the world. Any Scot will remind you that the credit for inventing it goes to a woman, a native of the port of Dundee, who, not wishing to take a loss on a cargo of rotting oranges, came up with the idea of cooking them up as preserves, using plenty of sugar.

Scones, the little cakes that come with afternoon tea, have their own story too: It is said they are shaped like the famous sacred Stone of Scone, on which all the sovereigns of Scotland were crowned. In the late thirteenth century, the stone was taken to England by Edward I; today, it rests in Westminster Abbey, beneath the chair used during the crowning of British monarchs.

Traditional haggis

ARE ALL SCOTTISH CASTLES HAUNTED?

In this land of history and legends, every plot of land has its old manor house or ruined castle. As night falls and the wind blows across the lonely moors, how can you help but believe in ghosts?

For centuries, on Scottish land, battles between clan chieftains ceased only long enough for them to unite against a common invader, be he Roman or Viking. A history so long and troubled encouraged the building of many castles across the country. Isolated fortresses or dark manor houses protected their inhabitants from both the threats of enemies and the harshness of winter.

Though ordinary Scottish people lived in modest houses, little stone buildings with slate roofs, the lords built themselves castles in such numbers that they are still one of Scotland's attractions.

Of all sizes and periods, used or in ruins, shrouded in mists—such as Glamis, where Queen Elizabeth and Princess Margaret were born and where Macbeth murdered Duncan—or perched on a rocky spur overlooking an austere landscape, most of them have a strange atmosphere, sometimes disturbing. And when you find out that, long ago, human remains were walled up within the dwellings, it's hardly surprising if ghosts do sometimes come back to visit the living!

But don't be afraid of meeting a ghost in Scotland: He'll talk to you nostalgically about the good old days when the Scottish nation was strong and knew how to cross swords with anyone who threatened its traditions.

Top: Glamis Castle, the most haunted castle   Bottom: Kilchurn Castle on Loch Awe

HOW DO YOU PLAY THE BAGPIPE?

It takes a lot of hard blowing to inflate the sheepskin bag that supplies the four pipes of the bagpipe. Three of them, by "droning," produce a background sound, while on the fourth, the melody is played.

The bagpipe—literally, "bag flute"—is not the only instrument the Scots have played in the course of their history. Gaelic bards sang ancient legends accompanying themselves on the harp. During evening gatherings, people danced jigs and reels to the sound of the fiddle playing wild tunes.

But the bagpipe was also an instrument used in combat. Its powerful "skirling" accompanied soldiers on the battle-field, where it was supposed to scare the enemy. Military tradition requires that Scottish regiments, whose bravery is legendary, always march to the sound of bagpipes.

In memory of past wars but also to defy the English government, which had forbidden their use, the Scots adopted the bagpipe as one of their emblems. Every Scottish city today has its bagpipe band, which plays in the parks in the summertime and so keeps the traditions alive. All these city bands meet once a year to elect the year's best bagpipe band.

In past eras, however, the Scots had no monopoly on the bagpipe; it was a common instrument all over the British Isles, as well as in various parts of France and Italy and probably elsewhere in Europe.

Left: Bagpipe player
Right: Bagpipe players on Argyle Street, Glasgow

WHY DO THE SCOTS HAVE A REPUTATION FOR BEING STINGY?

In every country in the world, city people say country people are tightfisted. It is true that in arid country places where life is far from easy, you have to know how to economize. But in Scotland, the criticism is unfair, because the Scottish farmer's prime virtue is, in fact, a sense of hospitality.

It's rather easy to get lost in the Highlands. In more than one region, there are few highways and they are little traveled. Not many people have lived there since the nineteenth century, when the landlords, or "lairds," cleared the inhabitants out in order to put sheep there instead. But if you meet up with a Scot, you'll soon be out of trouble, for, like many other peoples who care deeply about their traditions, the Scots understand hospitality. Life is often not comfortable, however, in the Highlands or the Hebrides Islands, but even if your host does not own much, there will always be enough to treat you properly as a guest.

You have to understand that the long, troubled period experienced by Scotland before it was joined to England regularly subjected its inhabitants to survival conditions. It was vital to be frugal then. Scots who traveled abroad lived the precarious life of emigrants. Out of all these trials, they have acquired a reputation for stinginess, more often than not unjustified. Perhaps this impression is confused by the reputation of some Scots as "canny," with a sharp eye for profit opportunities, a trait shared with others whose circumstances give them few sources of income.

Top: Pub atmosphere
Bottom: Little cottage on the moor

HOW DO CLAN MEMBERS RECOGNIZE EACH OTHER?

The fabrics we call plaids are almost a form of birth certificate in Scotland! The blend of colors, the size of the checks, the width of the stripes, and the way they intersect permit identification of the ancestral home and even the family of their wearers.

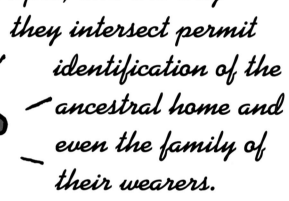

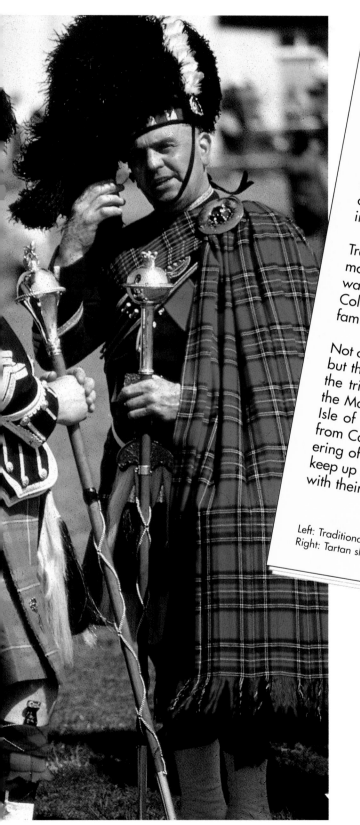

The clan is an institution that goes back to the Celtic period. It is, first, a large family, all of whose members are, in theory, descendants of a common ancestor; for instance, the MacDonalds are supposed to be the descendants of a man named Donald. But the clan is also a "party," with its own hierarchy, led by a chieftain. In feudal times, the clan lived more or less autonomously, owning its own lands and herds. Clans sometimes clashed with each other, reconciling only to fight off invaders.

Traditionally, the colors a clan might wear would vary. In modern times, the tartan, or plaid, became one of the ways by which clan members recognized each other. Colored according to a design that is individual to each family, the tartan acts as a sort of distinguishing uniform.

Not only is the meaning of the tartan still respected today, but the legend of the clans themselves has often survived the tribulations of history and family dispersions. Thus, the MacLeods gather in their castle at Dunvegan, on the Isle of Skye; some of them come from very far away—from Canada or New Zealand—to take part in the gathering of the clan. In Scotland, about fifty "clan societies" keep up the links among the most famous Scottish families, with their origins deep in the distant past.

Left: Traditional clan holiday
Right: Tartan shop in Pitlochry

HOW DOES A TRUE SCOT DRESS?

The kilt is a sort of knee-length skirt made of square-patterned wool and is worn with long socks. With a sporran— a leather or sealskin pouch— hanging on the belt, a tweed jacket, and a beret with a red pompom, it is the traditional Scottish dress.

The kilt is a fairly recent garment. In the past, the Highlanders wore a long cape—the plaid—cut out of the same fabric. During the day, it was thrown over the shoulder and fastened around the waist to make a cloak; at night, it was used as a blanket. After the defeat of the Highland clans in 1745, the British government forbade the Highlanders from using anything that might act as a rallying sign or mark of insubordination. Thus, they forbade their traditional costume. Later, as a sign of national pride, the kilt became the costume of every Scot.

Even today, the Scots like to wear this typical garment on special occasions or simply for walking or hunting. The full outfit consists of the kilt and its accessories: socks in which a small knife, a "dirk," is often hidden; the sporran; the jacket; and the beret. For many true High-landers, these are still everyday wear.

Prince Albert, Queen Victoria's consort, designed the type of kilt that is worn today (including in the Highlands); he wore it himself, and there were versions for sons, daugh-ters, and the queen. As it has had the right to do since 1604, the British royal family still wears its tartans—Royal Stuart, Dress Stuart, Black Stuart—particularly during frequent, regular stays in Scotland.

Above: The Grampian Band at Craigievar Castle
Right: Traditional costume

20

WHAT DOES THE MODERN WORLD OWE TO THE CITY OF GLASGOW?

Glasgow, with a population exceeding 689,000, is the largest city in Scotland. It is also one of the cities where, two centuries ago, the Industrial Revolution—which, for better or worse, was to shape our modern world—began.

It is to a Scottish scientist, James Watt, that we owe the ultimate perfecting of the steam engine. The use of this engine and the working of iron and coal mines in the area made Glasgow the world's foremost industrial city. Its blast furnaces produced steel for the shipyards, from which vessels set forth for the four corners of the British Empire to bring back the cotton that was woven in Glasgow's own mills.

A rich and powerful city, Glasgow was nevertheless to pay a high price for its industrial rise, for pollution and the poverty of the workers made life very trying in many working-class districts. Roused to indignation by the surrounding unwholesomeness and poverty, Robert Owen, owner of the mills at New Lanark, became one of the precursors of socialism, taking part in utopian labor reform.

Today, Glasgow, which has felt the full brunt of the economic crisis, is still a great industrial city. It is one of the world's electronics centers and also benefits from the refining of oil extracted from the North Sea. There have been enormous urban renewal and social improvement in the city, which won an award as a European Economic Community (EEC) "model city" for its architecture and progress.

Glasgow

21

WHAT IS A PUB?

The Scots enjoy going to the pub to chat and have a drink with their friends. But unlike the French-style "bistro," the pub is primarily a meeting place, rather than just a place for drinking.

The word *pub* is a contraction of "public house" (inn). It's an ideal place to get to know the Scots better. Although people do go there to have a few pints of beer or to enjoy a glass of well-aged whisky, more than anything else it's a "club" where people can meet their friends and chat after work. They play darts and cards, half-watching the television screen at the same time.

One should not be misled by the often austere outward appearance of the pubs. The atmosphere inside is welcoming: homelike, warm, and relaxing, especially after a long walk in the rain and the wind. A foreigner will more easily get to know the Scottish mentality in a pub, because pubs are places where talk becomes less inhibited . . .

Some pubs have two rooms—the public bar, where people drink standing at the counter, and the lounge bar, cozier and more comfortable. Once in a while, the "club" holds a concert. With the sound of the bagpipe, the songs, and the fiddles, one feels as if one has fleetingly understood the Scottish soul.

Top: Pubs are forbidden to children
Bottom: A pub at the foot of Edinburgh Castle
Right: Irish beers

22

WHERE WAS ROBINSON CRUSOE FROM?

Robinson Crusoe, whose real name was Alexander Selkirk, was a sailor from Lower Largo. He was marooned on a desert island for five years, an experience that was the inspiration for a very good story . . .

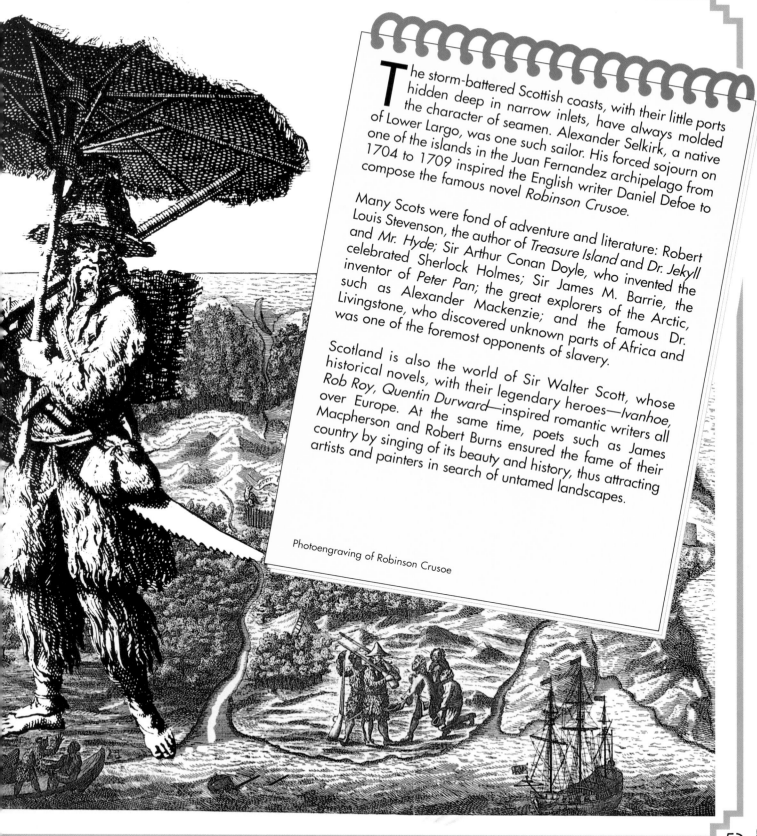

The storm-battered Scottish coasts, with their little ports hidden deep in narrow inlets, have always molded the character of seamen. Alexander Selkirk, a native of Lower Largo, was one such sailor. His forced sojourn on one of the islands in the Juan Fernandez archipelago from 1704 to 1709 inspired the English writer Daniel Defoe to compose the famous novel Robinson Crusoe.

Many Scots were fond of adventure and literature: Robert Louis Stevenson, the author of Treasure Island and Dr. Jekyll and Mr. Hyde; Sir Arthur Conan Doyle, who invented the celebrated Sherlock Holmes; Sir James M. Barrie, the inventor of Peter Pan; the great explorers of the Arctic, such as Alexander Mackenzie; and the famous Dr. Livingstone, who discovered unknown parts of Africa and was one of the foremost opponents of slavery.

Scotland is also the world of Sir Walter Scott, whose historical novels, with their legendary heroes—Ivanhoe, Rob Roy, Quentin Durward—inspired romantic writers all over Europe. At the same time, poets such as James Macpherson and Robert Burns ensured the fame of their country by singing of its beauty and history, thus attracting artists and painters in search of untamed landscapes.

Photoengraving of Robinson Crusoe

23

WHAT CAN YOU DO WITH PEAT?

Glasgow factories consume great quantities of coal, but peat is still the main fuel for heating the homes of Highlanders.

In the Highlands, where wood is scarce, the ground often consists of impervious rock, which does not absorb rainwater. The water lies stagnant in huge marshes overgrown by all sorts of mosses. As they multiply, the lower growth is smothered, dies, and decomposes under the water. The accumulation of decomposed mosses then forms peat.

Harvesting peat requires only a spade and a little energy: It is cut into slabs that are left to dry all summer before they are burned in the fireplace in winter. This is the way the Scots have always warmed themselves.

Though peat is also used as bedding in the cowsheds, it has, for the Scots, a mainly sentimental value: By filtering the rainwater, peat gives the rivers in their country their slightly amber tinge and the lakes their lovely dark tone.

Digging for peat at Quiraing on the Isle of Skye

24

DOES SNOWY HAVE ANY COUSINS IN SCOTLAND?

Snowy is a fox terrier who is more of an English type. His Scottish cousins are the Scottish terriers, with long black or brown hair, and the West Highland white terriers, with pure white coats.

The length of the coat, essential for protection from the harshness of the climate, is a distinctive mark of all the breeds of animal encountered in Scotland. Thus, it is said of the Scottish terriers from the Isle of Skye—chosen as an emblem by a brand of whisky—that they are a genuine embodiment of the Scottish character, lively, brave, intelligent, and proud. This assertion is made by the Scots themselves!

Of course, in Scotland there are other dogs, whose characters are somewhat quieter. Everybody knows the collie, the sheepdog made famous by Lassie, heroine of many adventures. Perhaps not as famous is the Scottish fold, a Scottish cat whose ears are folded down—probably against the wind!

The Angus (also a county in eastern Scotland) breed of cattle has a hairy coat, too, and the meat is as delicious as the pelt is shaggy. And Shetland sheep and ponies are no exception: They have lived so long in the Shetland Islands north of Scotland that its very harsh climate has certainly contributed to the thickness of their coats.

Top: Angus cattle
Bottom: White Westie (West Highland white terrier)
Right: Scottish terrier

25

HOW IS TWEED MADE?

The black-headed sheep, with its black head and feet, was raised in Scotland even in the time of the Celts. Today, it still roams freely over the Highland moors and on the coastal islands. Tweed is made from its wool.

Tweed (the name is also that of a Lowlands river) is a thick, warm woolen fabric resistant to wind, beating rain, and winter's cold.

Today, tweed is woven in industrial mills but always with local wool. A number of crofters continue, as in the past, **carding**, spinning, and weaving the wool from their own sheep, making it into fabrics of unequaled flexibility and lightness. The tweeds are dyed with natural pigments derived from bilberries, saffron, soot, lichens, and peat, the colors all in perfect harmony with the colors of the surrounding landscape.

The famous Harris Tweed is hand-loomed only by members of the Harris Tweed Association, all of whom live in the Western Isles.

The sheep live in semifreedom on the moor, watched from a distance by the shepherd and three dogs. They are rounded up only for shearing or for dipping in a bath of disinfectant to get rid of their parasites. The rest of the time, they graze on what they find where they are. If, while walking in Scotland, you happen upon a gate across the path, do not hesitate to climb over it: It is there only to keep sheep from wandering too far from their pasture.

Top: Spinner of Harris Tweed
Bottom: "Black-head" sheep

26

WHAT UNUSUAL GAMES DO THE SCOTS PLAY?

Every summer, the Highland Games are among the best-attended festivities in Scotland. The program includes such surprising competitions as hurling tree trunks or rocks! Weaklings stay away!

A dyed-in-the-wool Scot will not miss the Highland Games and will make it a point of honor to wear the kilt to attend them. Tradition reigns during this rather unusual sporting event: Old songs and lively folk dances are part of things, as is the nasal drone of the bagpipe to encourage the athletes.

And what athletes they are! Veritable giants in kilts, capable, in one test of strength, of hurling a smooth, round chunk of rock weighing a good 20 pounds (10 kg) over a distance of more than 30 feet (10 m). But the main event consists of throwing a "tree trunk." You have to be strong enough to lift at one end a 20-foot (6-m) pole weighing about 130 pounds (65 kg) and toss it into the air so that it comes down on the other end. It's called "tossing the caber."

If one wanted to compete, it would be best to have started in childhood eating the copious helpings of **porridge** that the Scots are so fond of for breakfast. . . .

Top: Braemar Royal Highland Gathering: tossing the caber
Bottom: Shot putting
Right: A champion of the Highland Games

27

WHY IS SCOTLAND THE COUNTRY OF GOLF?

The Scots may have invented golf. They certainly developed the game and spread it to the rest of the world. They've played it passionately for many centuries on the most beautiful courses there are.

The Scottish landscapes seem made for **golf**, which requires plenty of room. Scots took up the game with a passion. Their country offered the ideal terrain for the game: broad, uncultivated areas covered with short grass, spreading all along the coast between the seashore and the nearest fields of barley and turnips. The wind blowing from the open sea, by driving the ball off its course, made the game more challenging. . .

Though elsewhere in the world golf is still an activity reserved for the relatively rich, in Scotland it is a genuinely popular sport. Almost everywhere else, you have to be a member of a club or make a reservation to play on the golf links. In Scotland, on the contrary, the number of golf links—more than four hundred—makes it possible to play whenever you like and for practically no cost.

Of course, that is not the case for the "Old Course" at St. Andrews, a prestigious golf course located near the little fishing port of the same name. St. Andrews is a veritable temple of golf, where every great player should have driven the ball at least once in a lifetime.

Left: Golfer
Right: The Old Course at St. Andrews

28

WHAT ARE SCOTTISH RIVERS FAMOUS FOR?

With many of its fish-filled rivers and lakes still spared from pollution, Scotland remains a small paradise for fishing. But you have to be able to do combat on an equal footing with the king of freshwater fish: the salmon.

E ven though it may attain a weight of 20 pounds (10 kg) or more, the salmon is not the biggest of the river fish, but it is certainly one of the bravest. The fisher who hooks a salmon understands that the fight is not determined in advance. In Scotland, the story is still told of a huge salmon that was landed only after twelve hours of fierce resistance.

Thus, it often happens that, out of respect for so valiant an adversary, the Scottish fisher will release the salmon into the water again, just as a victorious wrestler helps the vanquished opponent get up. Basically, maybe the reason that the Scots like salmon fishing so much is that they have a high regard for a fish whose character is somewhat like their own.

Parallel with a type of fishing that is also a sport, salmon farming has greatly increased and has become one of the determining factors in the economic development of the Highlands. In 1980, Scotland produced 600 metric tons of fishery-raised salmon. Production ten years later had increased to 40,000 metric tons, an output that makes salmon farming, with its worldwide exports, one of the Scottish economy's success stories.

Fly fishing to catch salmon on Loch Tay

29

WHAT IS GROUSE HUNTING?

The Scots, who long hunted to improve their everyday food supply, now protect their country's wildlife. And to shoot the national game bird, the famous grouse, you need to wait for the right day . . . and aim true!

There is no hunting in Scotland today except on a few private estates, where the hunters, mainly foreigners, pay to shoot deer, snipe, or **grouse**. The grouse is a small, plump bird, whose dull-colored plumage is spotted with white and yellow; it is the favorite game in these regions. But you have to wait for the "Glorious Twelfth"— a special day indeed! It's on August 12 that the grouse-hunting season is declared open, an occasion not to be missed by a Scottish hunter under any circumstances.

To surprise the grouse, one had better not be afraid to walk for hours on end over the windswept moors, in search of a bird hard to aim at because it is so agile and quick. Grouse fly in small groups at low altitude and are clever at using the wind to increase their speed.

But it doesn't matter if one comes home with an empty bag, for in August, the sight of the carpet of mauve and pink heather in bloom makes a day on the Scottish moors a perfectly enchanting experience.

Left: Hunting grouse
Right: Grouse

30

DOES ANYONE STILL LIVE IN THE LIGHTHOUSES OF SCOTLAND?

The high cliffs of Scotland, jagged from the action of the waves and buffeted by violent winds, have always been a nightmare for sailors. The storms make the area look like somewhere at the ends of the earth.

From ancient times through the nineteenth century, the Scottish fishing ports became ever more flourishing trading centers. Whaling shops and freighters sailing under flags of every nationality traded in fish, purchasing primarily herring.

Though today the atmosphere of the ports is no longer what it was in whaling days, Scotland's lighthouses remain "such stuff as dreams are made on," still mounting guard along the coasts, to act after nightfall as guides to the sailors and intrepid fishers attempting to put into port.

If you happen to pass by there, don't forget to visit them. Most of the lighthouses are still kept by old sailors whose glance untiringly scans the sea. Some of them claim to be the last to have caught sight of the monsters and mermaids who lived in the ocean long ago.

Scottish lighthouses

B

BARDS: Celtic poets who sang in Gaelic of heroes and their exploits.

BEN NEVIS: the highest point in the Highlands and in Great Britain, 4,406 feet (1,343 m).

BRUCE (ROBERT) (1274–1329)**:** a gallant Scottish king. After claiming the throne in 1306, he spent most of his reign trying to free his country from English rule. Edward III finally recognized Scotland's independence and Bruce's right to the throne, as King Robert I, in 1328. He is an ancestor of Queen Elizabeth.

C

CAIRNS: mounds built of earth and stones, covering and protecting megalithic burial sites.

CARDING: untangling wool fibers before weaving them. In the past, this operation was done with the aid of a card, or brushlike tool fashioned from dried thistle-heads.

CELTS: group of peoples of the same civilization and language as the early Indo-European family. They occupied part of ancient Europe from the British Isles and Spain to Asia Minor.

CORNWALL: region of Great Britain in the extreme southwest of England.

CUMBERLAND (DUKE OF) (1721–1765)**:** British prince and general, born in London. Third son of George II. Vanquished at Fontenoy by the French, he was best known for defeating the Jacobites in 1745 and laying waste to the countryside.

D

DRAKKARS: square-sailed vessels with oars, used by Norman pirates and Scandinavian navigators. The name comes from the Scandinavian word for *dragon*, because of the emblem sculpted on the prow.

DRUIDS: name of the ancient Gaelic, or Celtic, priests. The Druids had religious, pedagogical, and judicial duties. They attributed mysterious powers to certain plants (for example, mistletoe).

E

ELVES: airborne spirits symbolizing air, fire, and earth, among other elements.

G

GOLF: sport in which a ball is driven by means of a club into holes arranged over a course, which is broken up by both natural and artificial obstacles. A full-length course of eighteen holes averages 5 miles (6.5 km). Some authorities trace golf back to a Roman game called *paganica*; others trace it to Holland. But most believe it was in Scotland that it probably developed into the game as we know it. The golf course at St. Andrews was founded in 1754 and is a leader in setting golf's rules and standards.

GROUSE (OR SCOTTISH LAGOPUS): bird of the tetra family. Brown with light patches, it grows to the size of a large chicken. Feathers hide its nostrils and cover the legs of most species to keep them from freezing. It crouches in the heather and makes a deafening noise when it flies away.

GULF STREAM: warm Atlantic current. It owes its origins to the Caribbean current and the waters of the Antilles Sea. By means of winds from the west, it makes western European winters considerably milder.

P

PICTS: early inhabitants of the Lowlands of Scotland. To defend Britain from their attacks, Hadrian's Wall, or the Pict Wall, was erected around A.D. 121.

PORRIDGE: boiled oatflakes.

PRESBYTERIAN CHURCH: a direct result of Calvinist doctrine, it was founded in Scotland by John Knox (1505–1572).

S

STUART, MARY: queen of Scotland, then queen of France by her marriage to Francis II. Widowed in 1560, she returned to Scotland, where she had to combat the Reformation and Queen Elizabeth I of England. Her marriage to Bothwell, murderer of her second husband, provoked an insurrection and her abdication. She fled to England, but Elizabeth had her imprisoned and eventually executed.

STUARTS (ALSO SPELLED STEWARTS): great Scottish family, from which the kings of Scotland came from 1371 until the Revolution of 1688.

W

WALLACE (SIR WILLIAM) (1270–1305): hero of Scottish independence. Born at Elderslie, near Glasgow. He led the insurrection against Edward I of England but was captured and executed.

B.C.
500

Settlement by Celts from central Europe
(500–200)

Conquest of Rome by the Gauls (390)

0

Roman conquest of the island of Britain (82)
Scots, Britons, and Anglo-Saxons repulse
the Picts (400–500)
St. Colomba and Christian evangelization
(late 400s)

Invention of paper in China (100)
Fall of the Roman Empire (476)
Founding of the Ostrogoth kingdom in
Malta (494)

500

Unification of the countries of the Scots and
the Picts (844)

The Vikings found a settlement in
Iceland (870)

1000

Annexation of Scotland by Edward I of England
(1296)
Scotland becomes independent and allies itself
with France (1328)
The Hundred Years' War, in which England
opposes France (1337)
Founding of the Stuart dynasty in Scotland by
Robert II (1371)

Marco Polo begins his journey to the court
of Kubla Khan in China (1271)
The Moscow Kremlin is mentioned for the
first time (1331)
The Black Death, an outbreak of plague,
claims 25 million victims in Europe (1347–1354)
The Kalmar Union: Eric of Pomerania
becomes king of the Scandinavian states (1397)

1500

Defeat of the Scots at the Battle of Flodden
(1513)
Scottish Reformation (1560)
James VI becomes king of Scotland and of
England, as James I (1603)
Act of Union, bringing England and Scotland
together to form the Kingdom of Great Britain
(1707)
Jacobite Rebellion against the succession of the
Hanoverian George I (1715)
Jacobite Rebellion led by Charles Edward Stuart
leads to pacification of the Highlands
by the Duke of Cumberland (1745–1746)
James Watt's steam engine patented (1769)
George IV becomes First Hanoverian king
to visit Scotland (1822)
First Reform Act (1832)
"Disruption" of Church of Scotland and creation
of the Free Church (1843)
Crofters War (1882), followed by Crofters Act
(1886), granting crofters security of tenure on
their lands

Ponce de León lands in Florida (1513)
Vasco Nuñez de Balboa is the first European
to sight the Pacific Ocean (1513)
Beginning of the Reformation in Europe (1517)
Victory of the English fleet over the
Spanish Invincible Armada (1588)
Jamestown settled (1607)
Carolina divided into North and South
Carolina (1712)
The city of Baltimore founded in
Maryland (1729)
Seven Years' War (1756–1763)
American Revolution (1776)
Battle of Waterloo (1815)
Abolition of slavery in British Empire (1833)
European Revolutions (1848)

1900
A.D.

Formation of National Party of Scotland
(1928)
First SNP candidate elected to Parliament
(1970)
Devolution Bill to create separate Scottish and
Welsh Parliaments for home rule defeated
(1979)

World War I begins (1914)
World War II begins (1939)

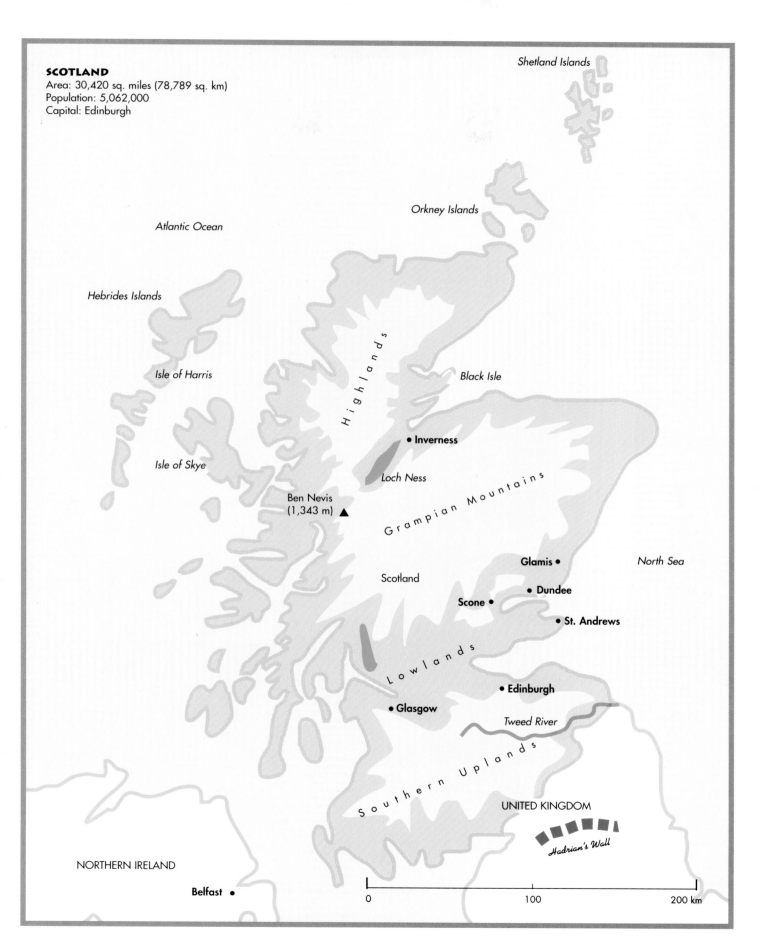

SCOTLAND
Area: 30,420 sq. miles (78,789 sq. km)
Population: 5,062,000
Capital: Edinburgh

Shetland Islands

Orkney Islands

Atlantic Ocean

Hebrides Islands

Isle of Harris

Black Isle

H i g h l a n d s

Isle of Skye

• Inverness

Loch Ness

Ben Nevis
(1,343 m) ▲

G r a m p i a n   M o u n t a i n s

North Sea

Glamis •

Scotland

• Dundee

Scone •

• St. Andrews

L o w l a n d s

• Edinburgh

• Glasgow

Tweed River

S o u t h e r n   U p l a n d s

UNITED KINGDOM

Hadrian's Wall

NORTHERN IRELAND

Belfast •

0   100   200 km

index

bibliography

SCOTLAND, FOR READERS FROM 7 TO 77

Begley, Eve.
Of Scottish Ways.
Minneapolis: Dillon Press, 1977.

Griest, Terry L.
Scottish Tartans and Family Names.
Annapolis, Md.: Harp & Lion Press, 1986.

Kellas, James G.
Modern Scotland.
London: G. Allen & Unwin, 1980.

Lye, Keith.
Take a Trip to Scotland.
New York: F. Watts, 1984.

Magnusson, Magnus.
Scotland's Castles and Great Houses.
New York: Harmony Books, 1981.

McDowall, Robert J. S.
The Whiskies of Scotland.
New York: New Amsterdam, 1986.

Meek, James.
The Land and People of Scotland.
New York: J. B. Lippincott, 1990.

Scotland in Pictures.
Prepared by Geography Department, Lerner
Publications Company.
Minneapolis: The Company, 1991.

Scott, Ronald McNair.
Robert the Bruce, King of Scots.
New York: P. Bedrick Books, 1989.

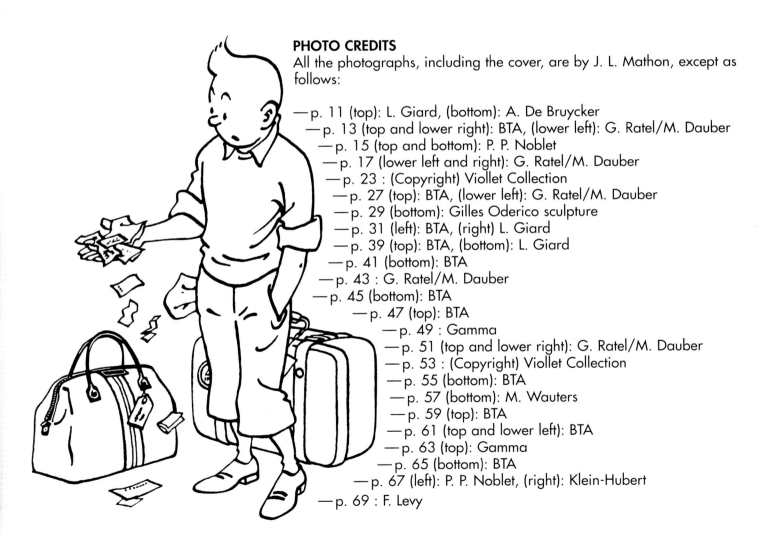

PHOTO CREDITS

All the photographs, including the cover, are by J. L. Mathon, except as follows:

—p. 11 (top): L. Giard, (bottom): A. De Bruycker
—p. 13 (top and lower right): BTA, (lower left): G. Ratel/M. Dauber
—p. 15 (top and bottom): P. P. Noblet
—p. 17 (lower left and right): G. Ratel/M. Dauber
—p. 23 : (Copyright) Viollet Collection
—p. 27 (top): BTA, (lower left): G. Ratel/M. Dauber
—p. 29 (bottom): Gilles Oderico sculpture
—p. 31 (left): BTA, (right) L. Giard
—p. 39 (top): BTA, (bottom): L. Giard
—p. 41 (bottom): BTA
—p. 43 : G. Ratel/M. Dauber
—p. 45 (bottom): BTA
—p. 47 (top): BTA
—p. 49 : Gamma
—p. 51 (top and lower right): G. Ratel/M. Dauber
—p. 53 : (Copyright) Viollet Collection
—p. 55 (bottom): BTA
—p. 57 (bottom): M. Wauters
—p. 59 (top): BTA
—p. 61 (top and lower left): BTA
—p. 63 (top): Gamma
—p. 65 (bottom): BTA
—p. 67 (left): P. P. Noblet, (right): Klein-Hubert
—p. 69 : F. Levy

BOSTON PUBLIC LIBRARY

3 9999 02847 645 3

CODMAN SQUARE

WITHDRAWN
No longer the property of the
Boston Public Library.
Sale of this material benefits the Library.